PETS' GUIDES

Kitty's Guide to

Caring for Your Cat

Anita Ganeri

Raintree

Raintree is an imprint of Capstone Global Library Limited, a company incorporated in England and Wales having its registered office at 7 Pilgrim Street, London, EC4V 6LB – Registered company number: 6695582

To contact Raintree:
Phone: 0845 6044371
Fax: + 44 (0) 1865 312263
Email: myorders@raintreepublishers.co.uk
Outside the UK please telephone +44 1865 312262.

Edited by Daniel Nunn, Rebecca Rissman, and Sian Smith
Designed by Cynthia Della-Rovere
Picture research by Tracy Cummins
Original illustrations © Capstone Global Library Ltd 2013
Illustrated by Rick Peterson
Production by Victoria Fitzgerald
Originated by Capstone Global Library Ltd
Printed in China

ISBN 978 1 4062 5057 2
16 15 14 13 12
10 9 8 7 6 5 4 3 2 1

British Library Cataloguing in Publication Data
Ganeri, Anita, 1961-
    Kitty's guide to caring for your cat. – (Pets' guides)
    1. Cats–Juvenile literature.
    I. Title II. Series
    636.8-dc23

Acknowledgements
The author and publisher are grateful to the following for permission to reproduce copyright material: Alamy p. 27 (© Catchlight Visual Services); Capstone Library pp. 11, 15, 23 (Karon Dubke); Getty Images pp. 7 (Antonio Perez/Chicago Tribune/MCT), 9 (Thomas Northcut), 17 (Steve Lyne); iStockphoto pp. 5 (© Louis-Paul St-Onge), 19 (© Michelle Gibson); Shutterstock pp. 13 bottom (© photomak), 13 top (© martellostudio),21 (© Alin Popescu), 25 (© Monkey Business Images).

Cover photograph of a kitten reproduced with permission of Getty Images (Lasse Pattersson). Design elements reproduced with permission of Shutterstock (© Picsfive) and Shutterstock (© R-studio).

We would like to thank Gemma Lovegrove, Veterinary Manager at Cats Protection, for her assistance in the preparation of this book.

Every effort has been made to contact copyright holders of material reproduced in this book. Any omissions will be rectified in subsequent printings if notice is given to the publisher.

Contents

Some words are shown in bold, **like this**. You can find out what they mean by looking in the glossary.

Do you want a pet cat?

Hi! I'm Kitty the cat, and this book is all about cats like me! Did you know that there are millions of pet cats like me? Cats are fun and friendly but you need to look after us properly for the whole of our lives.

Being a good pet owner means making sure that I've always got food, water, and a safe, clean place to live. Then I'll quickly become your best friend.

Choosing your cat

Cats can be different colours and sizes. They can have long hair or short hair, like mine. The best place to find your pet cat is at an animal shelter. They have many cats and kittens that need good homes.

Do you want a cat or a kitten? Kittens look cute but they need lots of special care and attention. You need to spend plenty of time playing with them. You might like to get an adult cat like me instead.

A healthy cat

Choose a cat like me with a clean, shiny coat and clear, bright eyes. It should also have clean ears and a dry, clean bottom. A cat that has a runny nose may not be very well.

Some cats are very playful and friendly. Others are shyer. Pick a cat that fits in with your family. A shy cat might find it difficult to be in a family with very small children.

Getting ready

It's almost time to bring me home, but there are a few things for you to get ready first. Here is my cat-tastic cat shopping list...

Kitty's shopping list

- 🐾 a cat bed or basket
- 🐾 **litter tray** and **cat litter**
- 🐾 a **scratching post**
- 🐾 a food bowl and water bowl
- 🐾 cat food
- 🐾 a brush for **grooming**
- 🐾 a **cat flap** (fitted in an outside door)
- 🐾 cat toys.

Welcome home

The day has come for me to go to my new home. You can carry me in a special plastic carry basket. Line it with newspaper and a cosy blanket or towel. You can use the basket later when you take me to visit the vet.

At home, put my bed in a quiet, warm place where I can sleep without being disturbed. If you've got other pets, introduce me to them slowly. Keep me indoors for the first three to four weeks. I'll need to go to the toilet in my **litter tray** until I can go outside.

Pick me up

Cats like me love to be stroked, especially on our ears and chests. If I rub my head against your hand, that's my way of telling you that I'm happy. Purrrr! But if my tail starts to twitch, it means that I'm getting fed up.

You can pick me up, but please do it gently
and use both hands. Put one hand around
my bottom and back legs to support my
weight. If I struggle, put me down carefully
on the ground.

Feeding time

I'm hungry! Purr-lease give me my dinner! I need food and water every day. You can feed me on dry or wet food, which you can buy from a supermarket or pet shop. Read the label to find out how much food to give me.

Kitty's top meal-time tips

- Grown-up cats like me need two meals a day. Kittens need three or four smaller meals.

- Please give me clean water to drink. Cow's milk can make me ill.

- Feed me in a quiet corner of the kitchen where I won't be disturbed.

- Put my food and water bowls well away from my **litter tray**.

Coat and claws

Cats are very clean creatures. I spend lots of time washing my fur. But you can help by **grooming** me gently with a soft brush. If your cat has got long hair, you need to brush it every day to stop its fur getting tangled.

scratching post

I need to keep my claws nice and sharp. Outside, I can scratch them against wood and tree trunks. Indoors, please give me a **scratching post** to use, covered in carpet or rope.

Play time

All cats love to play, but playing is not just for fun. It's the way we learn to hunt when we're outside. You can buy special cat toys but ping-pong balls, boxes, and cardboard tubes also make good toys.

If I live indoors, I'll need lots of things to play with. Otherwise, I'll get bored and unhappy. I'll also need safe places for climbing and perching. Outside, I can use trees and fences for doing this.

Indoor or outdoor cat?

Most cats like going outdoors to play and go to the toilet. Fit a **cat flap** into your door so that I can go outside. An outdoor cat also needs a collar and **tag** with your name and phone number on it. Make sure the collar is **quick-release** for safety. You can also ask your vet to fit a **microchip**.

litter tray

Some cats are happy indoors if you live
in a flat or near a busy road. But they still
need plenty of space to explore. They also
need a **litter tray**. Clean the litter tray out
every day. Wash your hands afterwards.

Visiting the vet

When I come to live with you, please take me to the vet for a check-up. After that, I'll need to go once a year for injections to stop me catching nasty diseases. Please also take me to the vet if I seem unwell or go off my food.

The vet will also treat your cat for **fleas** and **worms**.

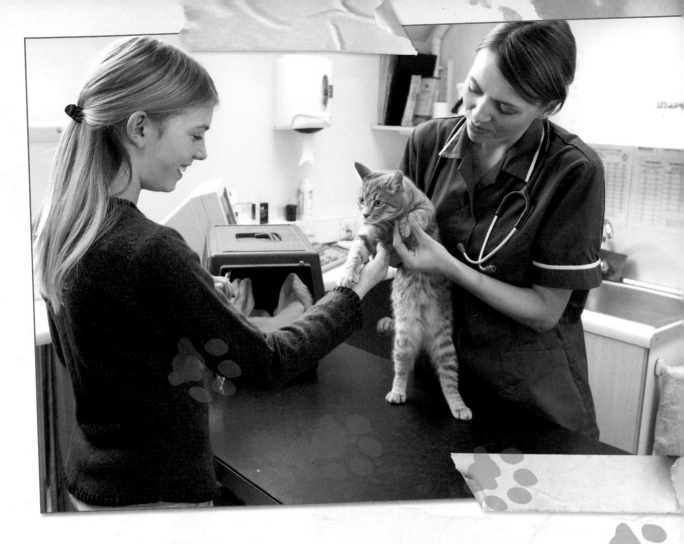

There are lots of unwanted cats and kittens. When your cat is four months old, ask your vet about having it **neutered**. This means doing a small operation to stop it having babies. It doesn't hurt and your cat will quickly get better afterwards.

Holiday care

If you go off on holiday you can't take me with you, so you need to find someone to look after me while you're away. Ask a friend or neighbour to visit the house every day to give me food and water.

Otherwise, you can put me in a **cattery**. It's like a hotel for cats. Each cat has its own pen with a bed and a **run**. Choose a cattery that's clean and friendly. Ask friends to recommend one that they have used.

Cat facts

- Pet cats are related to African wildcats.

- In ancient Egypt, cats were worshipped as gods. When a cat died, its body was made into a mummy.

- A cat's tongue is covered in tiny, sticky hooks. These work like the teeth on a comb when the cat licks and **grooms** its fur.

- In the wild, cats spend 6 to 8 hours a day hunting. Then they sleep for around 12 to 18 hours a day.

Helpful tips

- Cats rely on smell to tell them what is safe. A few days before you bring your cat home, take a blanket to the shelter. Your cat can get used to the smell and add its own smell. Then put the blanket in the cat's basket at home.

- If you introduce a dog to a cat, keep the dog on its lead. Reward it for staying calm. Give your cat the chance to get away if it needs to.

- Make sure the **scratching post** is tall enough for your cat to stretch out on and strong enough for it to lean on.

- Never leave your cat alone with wool or string. Your cat may swallow it or it may get wound around your cat's body.

Glossary

cat flap a flap in an outside door that allows your cat to go in and out

cat litter special gravel used to fill a litter tray

cattery a place that looks after cats when their owners go on holiday

fleas tiny insects that can live on a cat

grooming brushing or cleaning your cat's fur

litter tray a tray filled with cat litter where a cat can go to the toilet

microchip a tiny chip that is put under a cat's skin. It has a number that can be read by a scanner if your cat gets lost.

neutered when a cat has an operation that means it cannot have kittens

quick-release a collar that opens quickly

run an outside space with a fence around it

scratching post a wooden post covered in rope or carpet. A cat scratches it to sharpen its claws.

tag a metal circle that fixes to a cat's collar

worms worms that grow inside your cat and can make it ill

Find out more

Books to read

Cats (Pets Plus), Sally Morgan (Franklin Watts, 2011)

Complete Cat Care, Bruce Fogle
  (Mitchell Beazley, 2011)

Websites

www.cats.org.uk

Cats Protection is the leading cat welfare charity in the UK. It looks after thousands of unwanted cats and kittens every year.

www.rspca.org.uk

The website of the Royal Society for the Prevention of Cruelty to Animals has information about pets and how to look after them.

Index